Published by FourCP Publishing
PO Box 210312 Dallas, TX 75211

ISBN: 979-8-218-65085-8

LETTERS TO YOU

Interactive Prayer Journal

Rayla Blackmon

Edited by: Tori Broussard

THIS BOOK IS DEDICATED TO:

ANYONE, OF ALL AGES AND STAGES, HOPING TO GAIN A GREATER PERSONAL RELATIONSHIP WITH THE LORD THROUGH THE WEAPON AND INTIMACY OF PRAYER.

TABLE OF CONTENTS

INTRODUCTION

Despite growing up a "P.K." (preachers' kid), I did not always know how to pray or what to pray about. I assumed I should come before the Lord as perfected as possible with the right attitude and the right words, but I did not always possess those things; so writing, my outlet to everything, became how I weaponized prayer, and to my surprise, something beautiful was created out of that. It helped me go from formula to fellowship. From cowering to conversation. I wrote this (unknowingly) in the hopes of helping others feel the same transformative power of prayer, even if it starts with just a pen and paper.

The Lord's Prayer

"Our Father ....> ESTABLISHES RELATIONSHIP

Which art in Heaven
Hallowed be thy
name,

POSTURE OF REVERENCE AND KNOWLEDGE OF WHO HE IS

Thy Kingdom come, thy will be done on earth as it is in heaven.

---> ACKNOWLEDGMENT THAT THE WILL OF THE LORD SUPERSEDES OUR OWN + ESTABLISHES A HEAVENLY- FOCUSED POSTURE

Give Us this day, *our daily bread*
& **Forgive Us** our debts *as we forgive our debtors*.
Lead Us not into *temptation*,
but **Deliver Us** *from evil*.

ASK! MAKE YOUR REQUEST KNOWN TO GOD. BUT NOTICE THE LAYERS OF THE REQUESTS!

For thine is the Kingdom and the Power and the Glory forever.

ACKNOWLEDGMENT OF THE AUTHORITY AND POWER OF GOD

Amen."

AGREEMENT

*Reference: Matthew 6:9-13

Hey Folks, my name is Rayla!

First and foremost, can I just take a moment to thank you for your support in purchasing this journal? I never could have predicted that I would one day wear the hat of "author," but by faith in my Creator and my belief in the contents of this book, here we are! What you are about to journey through is a series of personal letters of prayer that I have written over the years. As life presents us with various nooks and crannies of circumstances, the topics of these prayers are broad, ranging from finances to relationships, and many things in between. Following each prayer is an opportunity to exercise your muscle of petition to God with a "Your Turn" prompt. After every 10 prayers, there will also be a moment of reflection where you will be given time to think back on how the last 10 days and/or prayers have impacted and challenged you, your thoughts, and notions coming into this. This book is not intended to shove Christianity down your throat, but it is the foundation from which all things were written. This book is not meant to force you to sit down and have a conversation with God, but is meant to reveal that whenever you are ready to, he's waiting with open arms and non-judgmental ears. Most importantly, however, this book is not meant to put a protocol on prayer, but to uncover the reality that it is simply a conversation that God longs for from you.

Now that we have covered the basic blueprints of this book, I would love to cover you, reading and partaking in this journey, in prayer. You ready?

"Lord, I come to you in this moment with a grateful heart. You have remained faithful, and your love, grace and mercy have chased me stubbornly. Lord, I take this time to pray for the one reading these words. Whether they have some knowledge of you, have been hurt or abused by religion, or know absolutely nothing about you, I thank you for their willingness of heart and boldness to pursue you anyway. I pray that the journey of this journal connects them with you on a more intimate level. I pray that through their time with you that you would reveal yourself to them in a new and fresh way - a way that is not filtered through shame, judgement and protocol demonstrated by poor representation, that has so often hindered people's approach to you. Love on this individual God, and allow them to see you for who you truly are - a Heavenly Father who died and rose for the WORLD, not just for a few. I thank you in advance for the freedom, peace and foundation that this journal could potentially create for the reader/writer. I love you and honor you in this moment...with love and gratitude I pray, in Jesus name,

Amen."

-Ray

SECTION
One

Prayer #1

Written on Sept. 16, 2018
"Dear Lord,
While reading Romans 1:16-25, I realized that I
would never want to turn into someone whose
thinking becomes futile and whose heart becomes
darkened. As hard as it may be at times, I want to
choose to give you the glory and praise that you are
so deserving of. Just as in any relationship, I am
sure there will be moments where I am hurt or
disappointed by your ways because they are much
greater than my own, and my finite mind may not
understand your infinite decisions concerning me.
But, I pray that you would allow me to see past my
flesh (carnality), and see you in everything – both
in what feels good and what does not . I pray that no
matter what I go through, you give me the strength
to lift my hands and give you the honor and my
trust. Tonight, this is what I pray for, knowing that
you and you alone understand my heart, and my
desire to never not give you what belongs to you. I
thank you and acknowledge you on tonight.
In Jesus Name I Pray,
Amen."

Your Turn!

Follow the Prompt Below

You have embarked on a journey of developing a more consistent prayer life by purchasing this journal. Now, I want you to write a letter to the Lord and express what you are hoping to gain from this experience. What are your hopes? Do you have any reservations? Simply share your heart…He's Listening.

Ready? Set. Write.

Now that It Is Written, Read it Aloud!

Prayer #2

Written on Sept. 10, 2018
"Dear Abba,
I thank you for this day that you have given me. I thank you for your provision. I thank you for your selflessness concerning me. I thank you for your mercies that are new every morning . I thank you for your grace. I thank you for your Word. I thank you for peace. I thank you for air. I thank you for health. I thank you for still allowing me the activity of my limbs, the ability to see, the ability to hear, to walk. I thank you for the sunshine and cool breeze. I thank you for family and your love shown through them. I thank you for the breath you have given me. Tonight, I just thank you Father...for all the things I take for granted. I thank you for an accommodating job (forgot about that one). But Abba, most of all, I thank you for just being a friend, a father, and an ear to listen when I need or call upon you. I thank you for granting me access to speak these words to you so freely. I love you Abba and pray a special blessing over my day tomorrow.
In Jesus Name I Pray,
Amen."

Your Turn!
Follow Prompt Below

We should **always** have something to be grateful for - no matter how big or small. Here is your opportunity to thank God for something. Maybe it's a new job, passing a hard test, or simply waking up this morning.
(Build the muscle of gratitude, as we will practice this a lot throughout L.T.Y.)
Ready? Set. Write.

Now that It Is Written...Read it Aloud!

Prayer #3

Written on Sept. 25, 2018

"Dear Abba,

My Lord. My Lord, I thank you! I don't know what you're doing, but I am in for the ride and trust your plans for me. I thank you on tonight and ask you for nothing. I simply thank you for my new car, for wisdom in finances, for the complete transformation of my husband into the man of God I know he is. I thank you for strength, for growth, for my home, for my children, for the turnaround in my father's heart and life. I thank you for the records that will change people's hearts, and for the books that will encourage the oppressed and depressed. I thank you for the continual outpouring of blessing and influence that you have placed upon me and my family. I thank you for platforms in which I have not seen yet. I thank you for the lives that will be forever changed. I thank you for your peace through every storm. I thank you for closed doors. I thank you for ways made when there seem to be none. I thank you for the fact that I am learning the value of thankfulness to you as my father. I thank you for hearing me, accepting me, loving me, and putting up with my craziness at times. I love you Abba, and honor you just for who you are tonight – a healer, way maker, promise keeper, provider, safe place, protector, and so much more rolled into one! See you in the morning!

In Jesus Name I Pray,

Amen"

Your Turn!

Follow Prompt Below

According to *Proverbs 18:21*, both **life** and **death** are in the power of the tongue. This means we have the power to speak death and life over our lives and the lives of others. In our last prayer, we practiced expressing thankfulness. Now, I challenge you to speak **life** and thank God for those things that you *cannot* see in your life yet. Is it a thriving business? Healing in your body? Whatever it may be, write it and then **speak it**...In Jesus Name.
Ready? Set. Write.

Now that It Is Written...Read it Aloud!

Prayer #4:

Written on Oct. 17, 2018

"Dear Abba,

I thank you for today. Tonight, I just say a special prayer over my loved ones and friends near and far. I pray that you would continue to work within them and through them. I pray that your will be done in their lives, and by the power of the Holy Spirit, I speak healing to the broken pieces, redemption from those places of loss, and wisdom in their journey, in the mighty name of Jesus. And it is so, with expectation, it is so. Holy Spirit, I simply pray that you would see me through tomorrow. Give me strength in my mind and body to move forward. I thank you Lord in advance and pray this in expectation of your hand to show up in my life and in the lives of those I love.

In Jesus Name I Pray, Amen."

Your Turn!

It can be quite easy to go to God selfishly, only bringing to him our wants and needs. But, what's more beautiful than this is intentionally going to God on behalf of others - a friend, a sibling, or a co-worker. Take this time to pray selflessly for someone else. Ready? Set. Write.

Now that It Is Written...Read it Aloud!

Prayer #5

Written on Nov. 25, 2018
"'I Am...' Proclamations
 I am Blessed.
 I am Beautiful.
 I am Intelligent.
 I am Healed.
 I am Successful.
 I am Bold.
 I am Set Free.
 I am Innovative.
 I am Necessary.
 I am A Blessing.
 I Am an Answered Prayer.
 I am Enough.
 I am a Child of the Most High.
 I am Anointed.
 I am Chosen.
 I am Patient.
 I am Kind.
 I am Productive.
 I am Unique.
 I am Purposed.
 I am a Role Model.
 I am Different.
 I am Special.
 I am Talented.
I am a Vessel to be used by God. In Jesus Name,
Amen."

Your Turn!

Follow Prompt Below

As we learned before, our words have power. Take time to the make your own list of "I am" declarations. I challenge you to not list these things through the filter of your insecurities or voices of others that may have hurt you, but by the hope of what you want to see in yourself. (Need help? Simply type *I am affirmations in the Bible* on your choice search engine). Ready? Set. Write.

I   AM

_____
_____
_____
_____
_____
_____
_____
_____
_____
_____
_____
_____
_____
_____
_____
_____
_____
_____
_____
_____
_____
_____
_____
_____
_____
_____
_____
_____
_____
_____
_____
_____
_____
_____

Now that It Is Written...Read it Aloud!

Prayer #6

Written on Oct. 2, 2018
"Dear Abba,
I thank you for this day. I thank you for your grace and mercy, for your love and strength. Lord, school is becoming so purposeless to me. I sit there not knowing why anymore. Although a degree sounds nice and fancy, I know it eventually will not mean anything. I know a piece of paper cannot provide the favor that comes from you! I have seen it, so I know I can make it with you as my qualification in anything. But Lord, am I supposed to be there? I do not know, maybe it is just the stress of it all, but I am really starting to wonder if this is your purpose for me. Am I supposed to be teaching children? Am I supposed to be in a nursing program? Is an educational system the only way to a promising career or my qualification to help people? Only you know the answers to these questions, which is why I come to you because I really do not know. Make it clear to me oh Lord. I love you Abba, and I thank you in advance.
In Jesus Name I Pray,
Amen."

Your Turn!
Follow Prompt Below

God is concerned about every area of our lives. In this prayer, I talked to Him about the frustrations of college. I was at a crossroads and knew to trust in the one who knew me the longest (**Jeremiah 1:5**), and who had my ending in mind (**Jeremiah 29:11**). Take this time to bring your concerns to Him no matter what they are, from relationships to career. Or maybe there are questions you are seeking answers for. I cannot promise you an immediate answer, but I can guarantee a present help in time of trouble (**Psalms 46:1**).
Ready? Set. Write.

Now that It Is Written...Read it Aloud!

Prayer #7

Written on Oct. 1, 2018
Dear Abba,
I thank you for this day. I thank you for
allowing mama to make it back home safely.
Tonight, I come in desperate need of your
wisdom regarding relationship, self-
awareness and this overall thing called
life. I know I still struggle with
insecurities, pride, and the inability to
communicate how I feel. But I know that
when you laid down your life for me that
you wore all the shame, pride, and
confusion that I sometimes feel.
Therefore, I thank you in advance for all
the strength and wisdom I will obtain. I
thank you in advance for my ability to
speak truth in a graceful manner. I thank
you in advance for these things knowing
that there is power, healing and
transformation attached to the name of
Jesus; there is no other name like Jesus,
therefore, Jesus is the name in which I
reach toward in confidence. I love you
Abba! I give you all glory and honor.
In Jesus Name I Pray,
Amen."

Your Turn!

Follow Prompt Below

In this prayer, there were parts of myself that I was ashamed of. However, I did not let that water down my faith in God nor His ability to help me through it. With that said, regardless of what you may see in yourself, take this time to 1) lay your character/habits/etc. before the Lord (honesty), and 2) speak victory over them (faith).

Ready? Set. Write.

_____

_____

_____

_____

_____

_____

_____

_____

_____

_____

_____

_____

_____

_____

_____

_____

_____

_____

_____

_____

_____

_____

_____

_____

_____

_____

_____

Now that It Is Written...Read it Aloud!

Prayer #8

(For the sake of privacy, names mentioned in prayer #8 have been changed)

Written on Sept. 22, 2018

"Dear Abba,

First, I just want to thank you for everything seen and unseen that you are doing in my life. I come to you tonight asking for wisdom regarding my finances. I know I have previously placed so much value in money...a lot of times too much. There have been points in which I have either been selfish with it, or not as cheerful of a giver as I should have been. Nevertheless, my heart is to really give my last to someone I care about and sometimes meet their needs before I meet my own. My friend and I's relationship becomes a little weird when it comes to money. I want to help Stacy in every way I can, but sometimes it feels like, and I hate to say it, but that I am being used or the only other one Stacy goes to when they need something. Am I wrong for feeling this way? Is there something wrong in me that is making something out of nothing? Is there a perspective change I need concerning money? I do not know. But I just need your guidance in this area of my life because it is difficult to navigate. This is a part of my life that I desperately need you in. I do not want money to become bigger than you, yet I also need it and truthfully like having it. There has to be a balance to all this. I may not have all the answers now, but I thank you for the revelation of all things.

In Jesus Name I Pray,

Amen."

Your Turn!

Follow Prompt Below

According to **James 1:5**, we are encouraged to petition the Lord for wisdom . A posture of willingness and humility presents the Lord with an opportunity to cultivate and prosper you. Here, I sought Him for wisdom in not only my finances, but my less-than-cheerful attitude when giving to others. Whether it be finances or something else, take this time to pray for wisdom in an area in your life you want to see growth and maturity.

Ready? Set. Write.

Now that It Is Written...Read it Aloud!

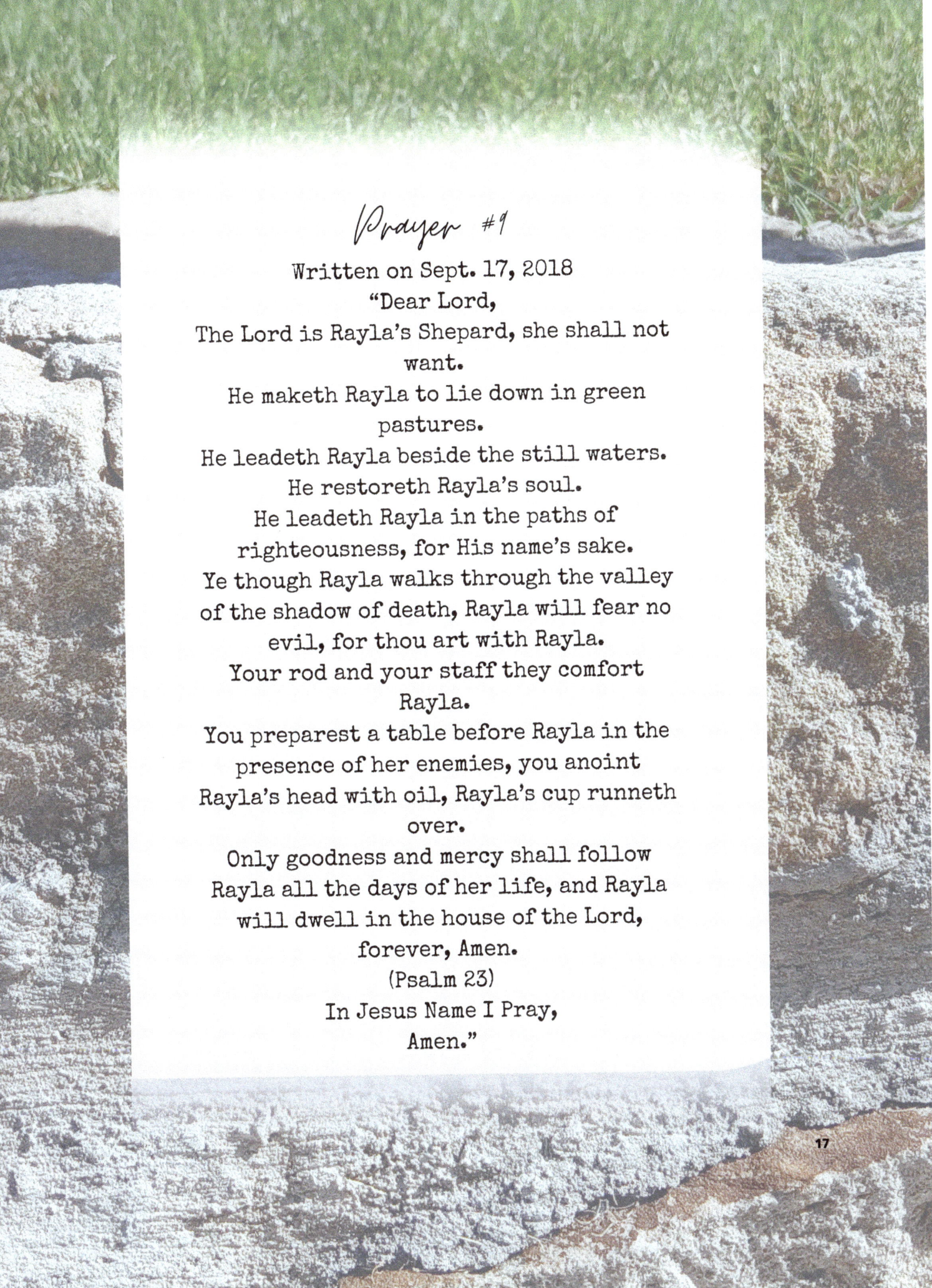

Prayer #1

Written on Sept. 17, 2018
"Dear Lord,
The Lord is Rayla's Shepard, she shall not want.
He maketh Rayla to lie down in green pastures.
He leadeth Rayla beside the still waters.
He restoreth Rayla's soul.
He leadeth Rayla in the paths of righteousness, for His name's sake.
Ye though Rayla walks through the valley of the shadow of death, Rayla will fear no evil, for thou art with Rayla.
Your rod and your staff they comfort Rayla.
You preparest a table before Rayla in the presence of her enemies, you anoint Rayla's head with oil, Rayla's cup runneth over.
Only goodness and mercy shall follow Rayla all the days of her life, and Rayla will dwell in the house of the Lord, forever, Amen.
(Psalm 23)
In Jesus Name I Pray,
Amen."

Your Turn!
Follow Prompt Below

Psalm 23 is an extremely powerful and commonly used passage of scripture within the Christian faith. Take this time to write out your own personalized Psalm 23 *using your name*. After doing so, speak it and believe it. Embrace the revelation that comes from it. How does reading it aloud make you feel?
Ready? Set. Write.

Now that It Is Written...Read it Aloud!

Prayer #10

Written on Oct. 6, 2018
"Dear Abba,
I come to you tonight father, not asking for
anything, but simply thanking you. I want to
thank you for being so accessible to me at any
time. I also want to thank you for everything
you have done and every door you have opened, as
well as every door you have allowed to remain
closed. Tonight, I claim victory over, and thank
you in advance for the week to come. I know I
stress and oftentimes feel overwhelmed with all
the elements of my life. But, I know that your
strength will get me through, your shoulder to
lean on will give me peace, and your ear to
listen to these words and the desires of my heart
will give me reassurance that you have got me.
Tonight, I only ask for forgiveness in all wrong
that I have done both knowingly and
unknowingly and I just thank you for the sweet
rest that is to come tonight. I love you Abba, and
I send your protective angels to cover my family
in this state and back home in Portland right
now in the name of Jesus. This I pray,
In Jesus Name,
Amen."

Your Turn!
Follow Prompt Below

As we did earlier in this section, let us conclude section 1 with the same attitude of gratitude. Before our first reflection, I challenge you to ask the Lord for *NOTHING*, but instead thank Him for *EVERYTHING*. Regardless of how you feel or the day/night you may have had, you're still here! If anything, thank Him for that. In my journey I've learned that thankfulness should never be circumstantial. Exercise the muscle of being grateful while sore. Ready? Set. Write.

Now that It Is Written...Read it Aloud!

REFLECTION

WHAT HAVE YOU
SEEN TAKE PLACE SINCE
COMMUNICATING WITH
GOD MORE?
(IF ANYTHING)

Open Thoughts

HOW HAVE
YOUR VIEWS
OF PRAYER CHANGED
SINCE BEGINNING
L.T.Y.?

SECTION
Two

Written on Sept. 26, 2018

"Dear Abba,
I want to say Thank you Lord, for all you have done for me. Lord, I love on you tonight. You are so worthy, so wonderful, so powerful, so mindful. You are Alpha and Omega, the beginning, and the ending. You are my keeper and shelter in times of trouble; you are my healing in illness, my strength in weakness, my wisdom in murky waters and my guidance on unsure roads. You are King of Kings and Lord of Lords. You are the way, the truth and the life (St. John 14:6). You are my Father in whom I trust. You are my shield, my comfort, my sword, my protection. You are my peace that surpasses all understanding. I give you all honor and glory tonight...Lord, I love you and give all thanks to you.
In Jesus Name I Pray,
Amen."

Your Turn!
Follow Prompt Below

Everyone loves a good compliment, right? God is no different. The Lord LOVES when we compliment Him. Expressing how amazing He is in your time of prayer is a form of *worship* and *admiration*. So, whether it's about how beautiful the sun He created is, or how faithful He is, take this time to compliment the Lord!

Ready? Set. Write.

Now that It Is Written...Read it Aloud!

Prayer #12

Written on Dec. 3, 2019

"Dear God,
It has been a while since I have written you a letter. I am sorry about that.
I have missed and needed these letters. It may sound weird, but in writing
you, I feel closer connected somehow – it's like I have the time to relay
every emotion and request to you in clarity. Truth is God, I am sad
sometimes. Some days I feel like I can do anything. But lately, my sad days
have become more common. Sometimes I am sad without a reason in the world,
which is crazy because there is so much to be thankful for. Like the love of
God ever flowing in this home, reaching the end of this semester,
approaching year 22, my trip to Oregon and so much more. Yet, here I find
myself in the pieces of a heartbreak.

For 2 years, you allowed an amazing guy to come and be a part of my life, and
although I am grateful for the clarity that came from the separation, my
heart is hurting. I need you to heal me Father. I know this is all a part of
the process, but it's not easy. Heal me oh Lord. Not just in my heart, but in
my soul. Uproot everything that has debilitated me emotionally. Daddy
hurts, little girl hurts, low self-esteem hurt, ex-boyfriend hurt. Whatever
it may be, I no longer want to be a carrier of it. You created me to carry
LIFE, not sadness, depression, and pain. Get rid of every hinderance that
has been placed in my path along the way. Give me your peace even more so
that it outweighs the distractions around me.

In Psalm 147:3, your Word declares that you are the mender of broken hearts.
Mend this broken heart, mind, and soul. Allow me to see the purpose attached
to my life. Distract me with the plans you have for my life. Engulf me in
your fire. Purify me in your flame. Cleanse me. Wash me. Make me and shape
me into the woman you have called and chosen. I write this/ profess this in
gratitude knowing that you have turned your ear toward me. I love you so
much Father, and decree that this prayer (letter) has touched heaven and
therefore, my request will be honored.
In Jesus Mighty Name I Pray,
Amen."

Your Turn!

Follow Prompt Below

At the time of writing this prayer, I was in the process of grieving a failed relationship. Despite knowing why the separation was necessary, that didn't take away the sadness and lonliness I felt. Take this time to get something off of your chest; a hurt, a pain, or bitterness that seems to linger. The Lord is more than understanding of our emotions. Don't make the mistake of hiding your vulnerabilities from Him. He cares! (**1 Peter 5:7**)

Ready? Set. Write.

Now that It Is Written...Read it Aloud!

Written on Oct. 11, 2018

"Dear Abba,
I thank you for blessing me with this day. I thank you for your continual love and guidance, and I thank you for just being you. Lord, tonight I come interceding for and bringing my home before you. I pray for the man of the house. I bring him before you right now in the name of Jesus. I lift his mind, heart, and soul to you. I pray that you wouldn't allow him to rest until he is hungering and thirsting and, therefore, seeking more of you. I pray that you would invade his privacy right now in the powerful might of your name. I pray that the worshiper in him will continue to tug on and pull on him until he has no choice but to lift up his eyes, words, and hands to you. Allow him to know you in a new way. Give him a fresh anointing. I rebuke and come against every spirit of depression, anxiety, control, anger, insecurity and hate that he may be harboring. I pray that through experiences you would fill him with the fruits of the spirit (Galatians 5:22). I pray that you would become his go-to, his right hand, and greatest friend.

Lord, I lift up my children to you. Not even knowing their names or faces, I give them to you right now. I pray that their footsteps bless wherever they go, that they will not fall into their surroundings, but that their surroundings will fall into them because people will see you in them. My kids will know you, love you, serve you and walk through this life standing on the foundation of their creator. I pray that their friends will be blessed by them. I come against every generational curse in the name of Jesus. My daughter(s) will not endure what I have endured; my son(s) will not have the same anger that I have. I pray for their souls even now and call them unique, gifted and blessed.

Lord, I pray for my heart and soul. I bring me and all my stuff to you. I bring my aches, pains, self-esteem, anxiety, sadness, pride, anger... I bring it all to you now. I pray that you would continue reconstructing me. Build me into a vessel fit for your Kingdom. I bind all generational curses that have found their way into this vessel in the name of Jesus. You cannot have me, for I belong to the Lord. You cannot have my home, for my home belongs to the Lord. Foul language you cannot have my words, for they belong to the Lord. You can no longer have my emotions and memories for it was all in the Lord's plan to get me where I am today. Lord, I thank you in advance. I praise you in advance. I smile in advance for I know the God I serve, and I trust the God I serve. Abba, my home will be made up of your servants. We will give you all honor and praise; we will acknowledge your presence in our lives, and we will live in a way that embodies our commitment to you! I love you and honor you on tonight Lord.
In Jesus Name I Pray,
Amen."

Your Turn!

Follow Prompt Below

At the time of this prayer, I had no husband or children. I did not know exactly who I was praying for, but there were desires I had in my heart pertaining to the type of covering I wanted in a spouse and things I hoped for my children. Take this time to pray for your home and your family that you either will create, or have already started. (*Update: In 2024, I married my best friend an answered prayer, Anthony!*)

Ready? Set. Write.

Now that It Is Written...Read it Aloud!

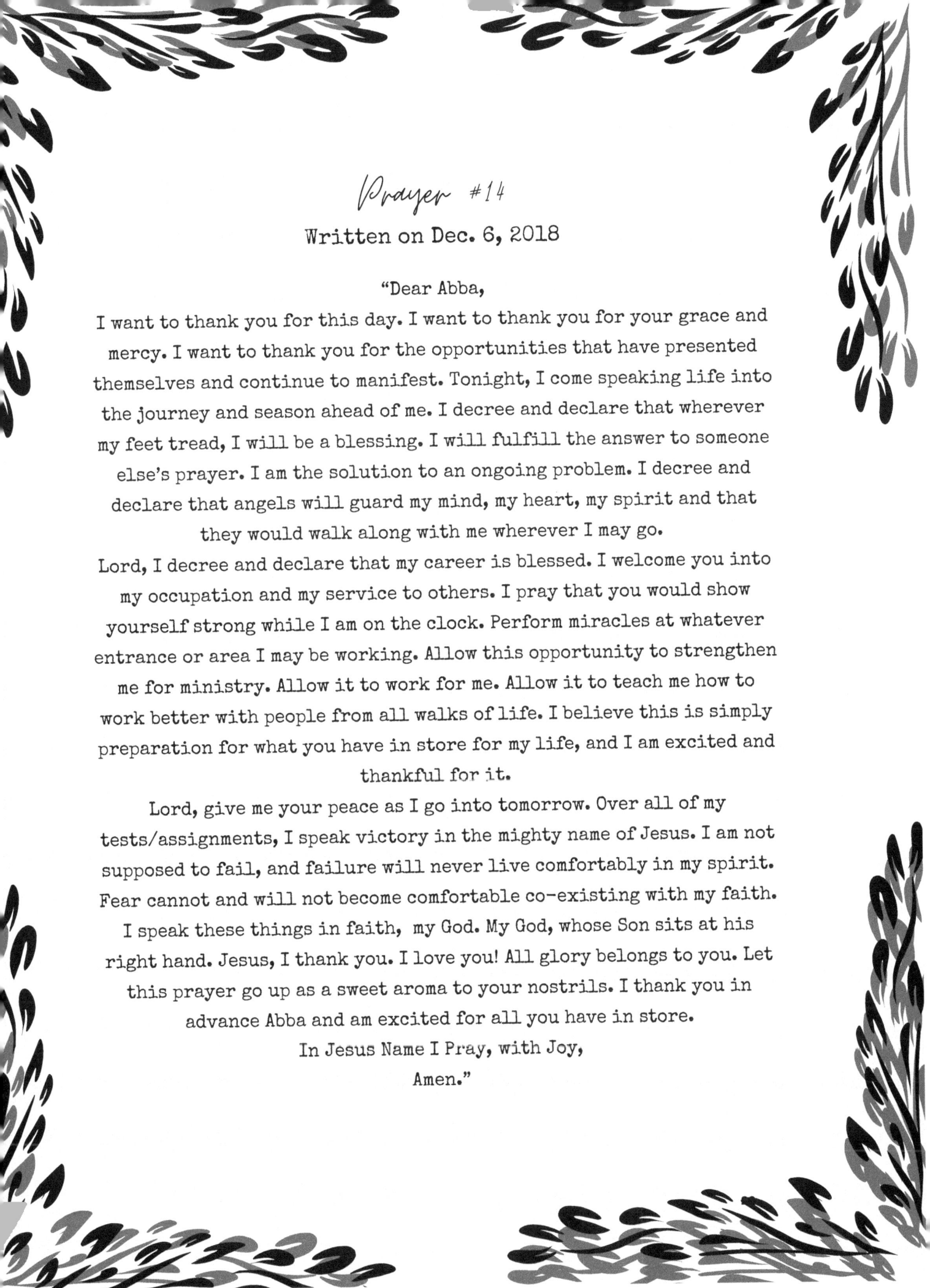

Prayer #14

Written on Dec. 6, 2018

"Dear Abba,

I want to thank you for this day. I want to thank you for your grace and mercy. I want to thank you for the opportunities that have presented themselves and continue to manifest. Tonight, I come speaking life into the journey and season ahead of me. I decree and declare that wherever my feet tread, I will be a blessing. I will fulfill the answer to someone else's prayer. I am the solution to an ongoing problem. I decree and declare that angels will guard my mind, my heart, my spirit and that they would walk along with me wherever I may go.

Lord, I decree and declare that my career is blessed. I welcome you into my occupation and my service to others. I pray that you would show yourself strong while I am on the clock. Perform miracles at whatever entrance or area I may be working. Allow this opportunity to strengthen me for ministry. Allow it to work for me. Allow it to teach me how to work better with people from all walks of life. I believe this is simply preparation for what you have in store for my life, and I am excited and thankful for it.

Lord, give me your peace as I go into tomorrow. Over all of my tests/assignments, I speak victory in the mighty name of Jesus. I am not supposed to fail, and failure will never live comfortably in my spirit. Fear cannot and will not become comfortable co-existing with my faith. I speak these things in faith, my God. My God, whose Son sits at his right hand. Jesus, I thank you. I love you! All glory belongs to you. Let this prayer go up as a sweet aroma to your nostrils. I thank you in advance Abba and am excited for all you have in store.

In Jesus Name I Pray, with Joy,

Amen."

Your Turn!

Follow Prompt Below

When I wrote this prayer, I was unexpectedly blessed with a 2nd job working at an arena. In this environment, I would have to interact with hundreds of people every shift. Despite nervousness, I did not allow that to muzzle my faith. Speaking success over yourself and whatever position you are currently holding is essential to seeing the hand of God work in your life. So, whether student or CEO, you give it a try! Ask the Lord to reveal the reason He placed you where you are!

Ready? Set. Write.

Now that It Is Written...Read it Aloud!

Prayer #15

Written on Sept. 10, 2018

"Dear God,
I thank you for this day and this moment. I love you with all my being and I love the feeling of actively building this relationship. Tonight, I come to you asking for wisdom. Wisdom in relationships, wisdom in school, wisdom in ministry and wisdom in growing in you and your plan for me. I am still learning, and I know that I have a lifetime of learning to do. I do not take for granted the gifting of evangelism and healing that I believe you have given me. I want to walk in these gifts with you right along with me...guiding my steps. I thank you for the dream last night and the interpretation that was presented—giving me gems of wisdom as I enter this next stage of my life. I pray that it continues. I love you, honor you, praise you, and give you all glory.
In Jesus Name I Pray,
Amen."

e·van·ge·lism
noun

1. Sharing the Gospel of Jesus Christ via preaching or personal witness to an individual or group of people.

Your Turn!
Follow Prompt Below

Remember that whole "wisdom" thing from Section 1? Yeah..let't run that back. Take this time
to ask the Lord for something that you need wisdom in. If not wisdom then perhaps patience,
or strategy. Whatever "It" is, be *bold* in petitioning Him for it!
(Hebrews 4:16)
Ready? Set. Write.

Now that It Is Written...Read it Aloud!

"Dear Abba,

I thank you for this day that was not promised to me. It shows me that there is still a plan that you have for my life. Lord, tonight I come praying over my relationship. I am so blessed that you have placed an awesome man of God in my life. I am filled every time we spend our time together. I will be honest though, and say that it is hard being long distance and our closest embrace being through our phones. However, I know that you know what is best in setting things up this way. I come to you tonight, oh Lord, asking you to cover the both of us. I pray that you would help the both of us on our individual journey's and cultivate us in the ways we need to push and birth out what you have uniquely put in us. It is difficult to navigate this relationship sometimes. Truthfully, I do not always know how to respond, encourage, or even understand him. He is so unique. He is peculiar. So, I pray that as his partner, you would equip me with what he may need of me and of what you require of me to be toward him during this time. Increase my kindness, my patience, and my capacity to embrace him. I will not claim to know the ins and outs of what this will be, nor will I claim to know with 100% certainty where this is going. All I know is that your strength and guidance is what I need. I thank you for lending your ear, and I pray this prayer knowing that you have heard me.

In Jesus Name I Pray,

Amen."

Your Turn!
Follow Prompt Below

I have always been a person who longed for the day I would meet and fall in love with *"my person."* However, as I matured, I learned that whoever it was that God chose belonged to HIM first, and that there were realities about me that rarely aligned with what I prayed for. Seldom did I take the time to look at myself and pray that God prepare me for what I longed for...*until this prayer.* This prayer allowed me to put myself and my then boyfriend, (now Husband), in the ring with the Lord and ask Him to equip and prepare us. Take this time, whether single or not/hopeful or not, to pray for "*the one,*" or even for the wisdom to know when he/she is not.
Ready? Set. Write.

Now that It Is Written...Read it Aloud!

Written on Oct. 21, 2018

"Dear Abba,

I thank you for this day in which you have blessed me with. I thank you for your grace and mercy that you have for me. Tonight, I come thanking you and interceding for the concepts you have placed within me. Lord, I decree and declare with the power of the Holy Spirit, deep down on the inside of me, that your will and purpose for my life will prosper. I decree and declare that every doubt, fear, and timid spirit be destroyed in the mighty name of Jesus. Make me a showcase of your glory. Give me the boldness to walk in proclamation of your glory.

Continue to give me the strength and tools to handle and hold this conception. Give me a sensitive ear to your voice; fine tune my eyes so that I may see with clarity. Continue to guide my footsteps and remove all distractions that may hinder my progress in you.

Right now, I plead the blood of Jesus over my anointing, ministry, gifts, talents, mind, heart, sacrifices, and assignment(s). Lord, I come kneeling before you and declaring: 'have your way in my life and give me the peace and strength I will need when I don't understand, when the road gets rocky and when my vision gets blurred.' Lord, I ask you to prepare me so that I may never turn away from your face.

I come against every plan, every attack, every agenda that is not like God, in the mighty name of Jesus. I speak these things into the atmosphere by faith. Lord, I thank you in advance for the way in which you are going to move in my life and in the lives of those I hold dear. This I pray in expectancy of your promises to be fulfilled.

In Jesus Name I Pray, with Love and Honor,

Amen."

Your Turn!

Follow Prompt Below

God has given every one of us a planned and purposed assignment and reason for being here. In this prayer, I took the time to pray and intercede for the reason the Lord saw it fit to put me in the Earth. Take this opportunity to pray over the purpose and assignment the Lord has given you - even if you are not completely sure of what that is yet. Ask Him to reveal you to you, all within His perfect and divine timing.

Ready? Set. Write.

Now that It Is Written...Read it Aloud!

Prayer #18

Written on Nov. 24, 2018

"Dear Abba,

I thank you for this day, for your grace and for your mercy! I thank you for the moments of laughter shared with my mother and for the beautiful people you allowed us to embrace on today. I thank you for your protection and provision as we went about our day.

Lord, tonight I come lifting my family to you (on both sides). I do not speak with everyone all the time, nor do I know their area of anguish, but you do. Lord, I decree and declare with the power of the Holy Spirit in me that every need be met, every hole of hurt be mended, and all areas of pain be healed. I come against any sickness. I come against any spirit that is unlike you. I come against all fear. I come against all generational curses dear Lord. I come against any roadblock that may be hindering or hurting the plans that you have for them. I pray that you would begin to remove hinderances, roadblocks, stumbling blocks, distractions; whatever "it" is so that they may be catapulted forward into newness.

I thank you for these words Holy Spirit, and speak them out of my mouth by faith. Lord, you have my family in your hands. Wherever there is a need, meet them where they are...in their kitchen, car, cubical, etc. I pray this prayer to you because I know you are the ultimate healer, provider, protector, and way maker. You are Alpha and Omega, the beginning and the end. Nothing comes forth without you first allowing it.

As your daughter, Abba, I know that there are things that I can petition and because I use your name, Heaven agrees. So, I say thank you for the ways you will create and the peace you will give where needed. I love you Abba, and all glory, honor and credit goes to you.

In Jesus Name, with Expectation, I Pray,

Amen."

Your Turn!
Follow Prompt Below

There is something so special about interceding for your loved ones. Take this time to cover your family, both immediate and otherwise, in prayer. Call them by name. Speak life over them. Truthfully, we never know what they may be dealing with internally, but we have a Heavenly Father who knows all and sees all things (**Psalm 139**).
Ready? Set. Write.

Now that It Is Written...Read it Aloud!

Written on Sept. 21, 2018

"Dear God,
I thank you. I thank you for your grace, I thank you
for your love...but more than anything I thank you
for the wisdom, peace and patience that you are
slowly teaching me to have. I am thankful for your
mindfulness of me and my weaknesses, and giving me
the opportunities to be different, see different,
and change for the better. Although the thunder
outside is a little scary tonight, I thank you for
the rain. I thank you for assisting me with that
test! Because I know that if it wasn't for you, I
would not have gotten through it. I ask for nothing
but continued learning and experiences of who you
are as my Father. Through this storm, I thank you
for greater understanding in all areas of my life,
in whatever capacity that may mean. I thank you for
your continual strength and guidance to maneuver
through the waves. I love you. I honor you. And all
credit goes to you...all praise goes to you. I thank
you Abba,
In Jesus Name I Pray.
Amen."

Your Turn!

Follow Prompt Below

Contrary to popular belief, it is necessary to practice thankfulness, even within the storms of this life! It is easy to go to anger, pride or seclusion when life is "lifing." Take this time to think of a moment in your life that was not easy, (*That moment may be happening as you write this*). Now, I want you to thank the Lord despite the rain and thunder that you endured or are currently facing. Know this - that it all must bow down at His word (**Matthew 8:28-33**). Ready? Set. Write.

Now that It Is Written...Read it Aloud!

Written on Dec. 23, 2019

"Dear Abba,

I thank you for today, for your grace, peace, and mercy. You are so amazing, and I cannot imagine life without you being a part of it. You are a good, good father and I am blessed to be your child. Tonight, I come with nothing but appreciation for every door that was not opened, for every friend that denied or betrayed me, and every plan or opportunity that did not work. I thank you for working even in my rejection - for using it as direction for me. I now look at rejection as an indication that I am on the course that you have laid before me. Lord, continue to teach me how to endure rejections, and to be steadfast in my faith when things do not pan out like I expect them to. Lord, give me the strength to partner with the pain that comes with rejection. Let it not take ahold of me, but me take ahold of it and see it as fuel as opposed to a sign of failure.

Lord, I know that I can only receive wholeness from you and that my self-love and esteem start with you. Make me whole. Cleanse me of all things unlike you and wash me daily through your precious Holy Spirit. If I do this on my own, it will be as filthy rags. Only your righteousness is what I am wanting and needing daily. I pray, decree, and declare this not only for myself, but for those I love. Make them whole Father. Allow them to see that you are part of a door closed just as much as you are a part of a way made. I love you Abba and thank you for your Word and those you have assigned to deliver it with such clarity and revelation. Continue to endow me with wisdom as each day passes. I pray this in anticipation of what is to come, and appreciation for lending me your ear.
In Jesus Name I Pray,
Amen."

Your Turn!

Follow Prompt Below

Rejection, regardless of its form, is something we all experience. However, very rarely do we look at a closed doors, failed business attempts or unsuccessful relationships as a *blessing*. Take this time to reflect on, and thank God for all the "things" in life that did not work, or that required going back to the drawing board. We never know what He may have been or is currently protecting us from, and preparing us for.

Ready? Set. Write.

Now that It Is Written...Read it Aloud!

What has this journey revealed to you about your relationship with God thus far?

From your experience using this journal, what are the benefits of consistent prayer?

REFLECTION

42

SECTION
Three

Prayer #21
Written on Dec. 21, 2019

"Dear Abba,

Lord, I first want to thank you for this full yet blessed day that you have allowed me to have. You are so mindful and loving toward me and for that, I honor you. You are Alpha and Omega, the beginning and the end. You are King of Kings and Lord of Lords. You are the son of David, the one and only true Father. You are my healer and my strength. From you and you alone come my righteousness and I am thankful just to know your name. Abba, tonight I come to decree and declare success and clearer vision concerning the businesses and books that you have placed inside of me to do. Lord, I lay at your throne "Academy X," "Given to Give," "The 4 Corners Project," and "When Life Speaks" in the mighty name of Jesus. Lord, all these ideas belong to you. I am simply the carrier. I decree and declare that these ideas would be the birthing place for other young visionaries. I decree and declare that in the right timing, these ideas will be on shelves and in full operation. I decree and declare that these seeds will be so productive that a legacy is left for my children's children! I decree and declare that no weapon, plot, or plan of the enemy will prosper against my assignments. I decree and declare that I am more than capable and armed to carry these seeds. I speak these things in anticipation and faith that Heaven is backing me up even now. Lord, I thank you in advance knowing you have lent me your ear. I pray that my spiritual senses are heightened in the coming year (days). Allow my taste, touch, smell, sight, and hearing to elevate to a frequency so clear that I can feel when and where to move in order to follow the steps that you have already ordained for me to take. I love you, honor you and know that without you, I am nothing.

In Jesus Mighty and Amazing Name, I Pray,

Amen."

Your Turn!

Follow Prompt Below

Interestingly enough, when I wrote this I had no idea that *Letters to You: Interactive Prayer Journal* should've been added to the list. What I assumed was an easier way to pray, by grace, turned it into a tool to introduce others to the power of prayer. Who would have thought? With this said, despite our ambitions as human beings, there are dreams and visions that are given to us directly from the Lord himself. Take this time to pray over, cover and submit every business model, book title, and aspiration before the Lord.
Ready? Set. Write.

Now that It Is Written...Read it Aloud!

Prayer #22

"Dear Abba,

Thank you for this day that you have given me. Thank you for your love, peace, grace, and mercy that echoes in and throughout my life daily. I thank you for your word that continues to be a lamp to my feet and light to my path (Psalm 119:105). Lord, tonight I come requesting that you take every ounce and inch of pride out of me. I do not want to operate from a spirit of false humility, nor an impure state of mind concerning myself and those around me. Lord, I have seen the ugly head of pride weave itself in and throughout my family. However, tonight I decree and declare that it stops with me. Allow me to see and love myself and others through your lenses. Help me to uproot the habit of comparing myself (my worth) to what's on the outside of myself. Help me to only compare who I am today with who you have called me to be tomorrow. Overall, God I know that with you involved anything is possible. I pray that with each day that passes, you would remind me in someway that this life I live is not for me and myself alone, but for a far greater and miraculous purpose. Lord God, I pray that you would allow humility to be the grounds in which I operate from, and the spirit in which all I bring forth comes from. Keep me in low places so that I may grow to appreciate them and, when on a hilltop, see their significance. My Abba, I am forever yours. You are my Father and should therefore see a resemblance of you in me. I pray that resemblance becomes clearer and stronger with each passing day. In Jesus Mighty and Awesome Name, I Pray, Amen."

Your Turn!

Follow Prompt Below

In this prayer, I brought a few of my greatest challenges to the Lord. Be it pride or low self-esteem, the Lord can help us in any situation we invite Him into. We must realize and remember that He is genuinely concerned about our struggles. We cannot be afraid to expose any inadequacies before Him (**2 Corinthians 12:9**). Try it for yourself.

Ready? Set. Write.

Now that It Is Written...Read it Aloud!

Written on Jan. 4, 2020

"Dear Abba,

Hi Father! I know I sometimes slack with these letters, so I am sorry about that. But I am thankful to you, who you are, and who you have been to me. You have and continue to be our helper, comforter, provider, and healer. Your grace and mercy have carried us, and your peace has soothed us beyond comprehension. I thank you. You are so great and mighty. There is not and will never be anyone like you and I am blessed to call you friend. Tonight, I come interceding for my mother and her body. In the mighty name of Jesus, I decree and declare that she will be made whole and with the blood of Jesus I come against every attack that is trying to invade her body. God, you are the same God that gave sight to the blind, restored the lepers, and raised the dead (Luke 7:22). My confidence is solely in your healing power and I believe that from the crown of her head to the soles of her feet, both internally and externally, she is made whole! Tonight, I also come lifting up my father. I do not pray for him much, but tonight I intercede for his health and his mind. Lord, restore my father. Reach into the very crevices of his heart that only you can reach and bring to him true freedom, healing, and peace. I pray for my brother on tonight too Abba. I do not know nor see all the details, but you do. Touch him Lord, protect him and revive the Man of God that has been muffled through circumstances. Lord, you know the needs of my family, but you also know the purpose that you have strategically planned for each of our lives. I pray that each one of those purposes are fulfilled regardless of the journey and how difficult it might be. I decree and declare that my family will live out the purpose that has been assigned to their lives. No demon, devil, or evil spirit will interfere with their purpose because as they have covered me, I cover them with the blood of Jesus. The blood that cleanses, protects, and purifies. Lord, I thank you for lending your ear and I have faith that you have heard and honored this plea.
In the Mighty and Righteous Name of Jesus,
Amen."

Your Turn!

Follow Prompt Below

At the time of this prayer, I did not know that I, along with multiple members of my family would test positive for Covid-19 just months later. At the time of this prayer, I did not know what a global pandemic looked like. At the time of this prayer, I did not know that I would watch my father suffer multiple heart attacks just a short time later. So, here we are again, lifting up our families. Take this time to pray over your own. Call out their names and **practice** the power of intercession.
Ready? Set. Write.

Now that It Is Written...Read it Aloud!

Prayer #24

"Dear Lord,

Tonight, I ask you for nothing.

I just want to say thank you and

that I love you.

In Jesus Name I Pray,

Amen."

Your Turn!

Follow Prompt Below

Yep, that is right! A classic 1-2 liner. Sometimes, a thankful heart and open ears is all we need to have. Take this moment to write something short and sweet to the Lord. Every prayer is not required to be long and wordy (**Matthew 6:5-14**). Some prayers are only a few words, a smile, or even tears. Ready? Set. Write.

Now that It Is Written...Read it Aloud!

Prayer #25

"Dear Abba,

I thank you for this day. I thank you for all the many ways that you have made and the continual peace you give me during life's hardships. I never would have imagined that my father would be dealing with such traumatizing health issues. The heart is his engine...yet it has been attacked. The medications meant to help him come with effects that seem counterintuitive to his healing. It's hard to watch, especially when I am not able to physically be there with him. I want to walk by his side, bring him his food, and assume a role that requires him to do nothing but rest. But that is not my reality. All I can do is what I am doing right now, pray and intercede for his healing. Lord, although doctors and medical professionals are no doubt a gift to this world, I do not look to them as my father's healer. I look to you as my father's healer. Lord, you know the ins and outs of this man and all of what he needs right now. Be all that he needs Abba. You are the great physician (Isaiah 53:5), and I know that if you can heal me and my family from Covid-19, you can heal his heart indefinitely. I know that if you can take my mother in and out of multiple surgeries successfully, you can heal every system and major organ in his body. His illness is not beyond you. His issues are not beyond you. All that we face is so very often beyond us, and that is why we look to you for direction and restoration. Introduce your "super" to our very natural situation. Make him whole Father, in a way that even surprises him. I pray for a favorable outcome out of this "necessary inconvenience." Nevertheless, I do not do this without acknowledging your will for his life. Despite what I want, Lord let your will prevail. However long that takes, however painful it may be, let your will supersede my desires, and give me the peace to handle whatever that will is. Cover me and my brother now Lord, as we enter this arena in which we have never been. We know that as we age, our parents do as well, and we know that there are things that can arise during that time. So, I pray that supernatural strength, peace, joy, and love would overtake my family. Show us you in a way that we all individually need and understand. I pray this knowing that heaven has heard me, and that you have selflessly lent me your ear, and for that I am extremely thankful.

In Jesus Mighty Name I Pray,

Amen."

Your Turn!

Follow Prompt Below

As we get older, we experience changes, both good and bad, that can be very overwhelming. In this case, it was the turn of my father's health. I did not anticipate possibly losing a parent at only 23, but life happened. Take this time to specifically cover your *parent(s)*. If your parents are no longer with you, pray for someone who you know is a parent, or someone you look to as a parental figure. Most importantly, if you are currently at odds with your parent(s), or have found yourself battling unforgiveness towards them, invite the Lord into that space.

Ready? Set. Write.

Now that It Is Written...Read it Aloud!

Prayer #26

Written in 2020

"Dear Abba,
Lord, tonight I come interceding for this country. Lord, I come asking for your peace over this nation right now in the mighty name of Jesus. As people rest on tonight Lord, change their hearts and minds concerning this panic. Rest your spirit over this nation. Remind your people that you, the God Almighty, are in control. I come against every ungodly force and spirit of greed, selfishness, fear and doubt right now in the wonderful and powerful name of Jesus. We are in a season where light and darkness can no longer coexist. So, I serve notice to the Kingdom and principalities of darkness to loosen its hold right now in the name of Jesus, for the Blood of Jesus is a sword to your neck. For it is written that you have already been defeated and nothing you do will change that. I decree and declare that all plots and plans in place to derail the works of my Lord bow down under the miraculous name of our Lord and Savior.

For in my God, there is victory, peace, healing, deliverance, and freedom. Lord, have your way. Do as you see fit in this time! You are all-knowing and nothing happens that you do not first allow. I thank you for a clear heart and peace of mind. I thank you for keeping and protecting my loved ones, oh God. I thank you for never leaving nor forsaking your children. I thank you in advance for showing yourself mightily and strong in this world. This world is crying for a savior. This world needs you, my God. Meet them in their dreams, speak through their children, and embrace them in their darkest of places. I love you Abba and believe that you have heard this plea. I thank you for lending an ear and for the dispatching of your angels to back me up!

In Jesus Name with Gratitude and In Expectation I Pray, Amen."

Your Turn!
Follow Prompt Below

As we all know, 2020 was an absolutely unforgettable year for the entire world. Here, I learned that praying for our communities, state, and nation are so important, regardless of our feelings toward those we're praying for. Take this time to intercede for our world leaders, from the national level to the local level. Pray for the release of Godly wisdom and for the Lord to show Himself strong in our elected officials (**Isaiah 9:6**). Trust me when I say, they need it more than we think.

Ready? Set. Write.

Now that It Is Written...Read it Aloud!

Prayer #27

Written on Jan. 1, 2020

"Dear Abba,
I made it! I made it to 2020 and could not be more grateful and amazed by your grace and mercy. It is you, Abba, that has kept me. It is you that has protected me and my family from dangers seen and unseen. It is you Father that has kept us and molded us and brought us through to this point. For that, I thank you! Lord, going into this new year, I want to surrender and relinquish old thought patterns, fears and 'gunk' that has stuck itself to me. I need all that you have in store for me, and do not want to sabotage it in any way. Therefore, God I ask that everything that has a purpose attached to it connect itself to me and everything that has no purpose, disconnect me from it. Lord, help me to become bold enough against anything old that may try to resurface. Dress me, oh Lord, with all I need in this 'right now' season. Lord brace my heart and my mind for all of what is to come. Wrap your arms around me Abba, because without you, this journey is impossible. Lord, increase my spiritual senses so that I would not be driven by my natural ones. Keep me in a humble posture so that I can clearly see the realities of mountaintop moments. Purge me oh Lord, of any unclean thing that is not like you, that I may be poured into by you, and you alone. Renew my mind because I know that my thoughts direct my feet. Order my steps God, so that I may walk into the plans that have already been predestined. I do not want to miss you in this season oh Lord, and I pray that I would not rest until I get into the position to be taught and corrected. Help me to not get easily offended. Help me to not judge others based on my own insecurities. Continue to fill me with your Holy Spirit so that I may walk and talk in your image and likeness! Convict me as needed. Cleanse me as needed so that I may give out from a place of wholeness and be in the necessary posture to receive all that you have already scheduled to give. I pray this prayer in confidence and faith that you have heard me. I thank you for lending me your ear.
In Jesus Mighty Name I Pray, In Expectation,
Amen."

Your Turn!
Follow Prompt Below

The greatest sacrifice we can offer to the Lord is a willing heart and obedience. What are you willing to give up and relinquish into His hands? Your business? Your children? Your plans? Take this time to offer something to the Lord. Give Him creative control over your life, and express to Him those things about you that you want Him to help you in.
Ready? Set. Write.

Now that It Is Written...Read it Aloud!

Written on Aug. 11, 2021

"Dear Abba,

I thank you on this morning. I thank you for waking me up in my right mind and I thank you for your Word and instruction. You know, today's verse of the day seemed to have last night in mind. It's sad to think that after so many years, masturbation and pornography is still something that shows up in my life. But, as long as I am in connection with you while dealing with these ups and downs, then that's all that matters. It is then that I am confident that it will not always be like this. I still decree and declare healing in my mind and body over masturbation and pornography right now in the name of Jesus. I am healed and I am delivered in spite of what it may look like. Lord, I know that I find myself knocking on doors that I have no business opening, so I pray that in those moments, the Holy Spirit would hold me, and remind me of the words you've made available to me about avoiding seduction and the ramifications AGAINST MYSELF if I refuse (1 Corinthians 6:18). Lord, I bring this matter to you because I know you are the only one capable of completely taking this desire from me. Today, Lord I also lift up my ability and capacity to listen. Why am I so defiant? Why did starting the phrase with 'you need to...' bother me so much? I know it may take some digging to find out the answer to these questions on my part, but Lord, whenever you are willing, please reveal these things to me. I want to be able to walk in humility that I may take heed to sound council. Also, as I write/read this to you, I lay my hand on my own self and decree healing over this recurring headache in the name of Jesus. For you have gifted me the spirit of power, love and a sound mind. So, I put a demand on my soul, my thoughts and my body to come into alignment with the healing you have destined me to have. There is no other God like you, Lord. There is no other name that stands up to yours. There is no false idol, sickness, disease, devil nor demon that you have not already defeated. I rest well in that understanding. I love you Abba and thank you for lending your heart and ear to me this morning. In Jesus Mighty name I pray, Amen.

Your Turn!
Follow Prompt Below

In this letter, I participated in my own journey of healing from three things in particular:
- A recurring migraine that would not let up (likely stress related)
- A newly found defiance I had in listening to sound council (**Proverbs 19:20**)
- A more than decade long addiction to pornography and masturbation (**1 Corinthians 6:18**)

Although all different, all of which were things I tried to handle on my own, as we all often try to do. But no matter how simple or impossible something may seem, the Lord is not intimidated nor surprised by anything we do. Take this time to bring your dirt to the Lord. Where do you need healing? What cross are you trying to bear in private? Bring it to Him!
Ready? Set. Write.

Now that It Is Written...Read it Aloud!

"Dear Abba,

I come to you tonight thankful. There are so many changes in life that can be overwhelming, but I try not to let them interfere with my gratitude toward you. It seems like on one spectrum, I am coming into all these new and exciting things, like relationships and being able to further my education, while on the other hand, I am witnessing death after death close to home, and watching my father suffer like never before in his body from afar. This is a part of my life that is 'beautifully horrific.' I do not always know what to pray for. I do not always know when to relax and celebrate. This is a place that I have never been nor thought I would ever be. But I guess the thankfulness emerges in me knowing that all things do work together for my good (Romans 8:28). It arises when I remember that you knew what every one of my days would look like before I got here to live them out (Psalm 139:16). I find comfort in knowing that you lead me besides still waters and that your rod and staff are there with me (Psalm 23:2-4). I never knew being overjoyed and overwhelmed was a possibility. But in it, I know that you are still God and that you never promised ease in this journey of life.

So, Lord, with my hands open, I lift it all to you. I lift the grief of those I love, the frustrations of 'what's next,' the unknowns of my family, and the protection and preparation of my heart. I cast it to you. Your Word instructs me to cast all cares to you (1 Peter 5:7) – so I willingly do so and ask that you give me the strength to keep it that way. As you know, we all too often lay things down just to pick them back up. Nevertheless, despite life's beautiful waves and violent winds, I continue to put my faith in you. I continue to find something, even in this moment to be thankful for. I thank you for letting me hear my father's voice again, even if it is from a hospital bed. I thank you for a best friend that never seems to get tired of me. I thank you for a flexible job that allows me to handle my responsibilities at home. I thank you for my family. I thank you for your strength that gets me through. I thank you for breath in my body. Thank you for allowing be to be thankful when I could be bitter. It is only you that enables this within me, and I thank you. I love you. I honor you.

In Jesus Mighty Name I Pray,

Amen."

Your Turn!

Follow Prompt Below

Life has a way of letting us experience a little bit of heaven and a little bit of hell all at the same time. This was a time for me. The night I wrote this, I had just gotten a call informing me that my dad had being admitted to the hospital for the 4th or 5th time within an eight or so week period. It was tough, but the Holy Spirit gave me peace through it (**Philippians 4:4-7**). Take this time to choose gratitude and THANK GOD ANYWAY!
Ready? Set. Write.

Now that It Is Written...Read it Aloud!

Prayer #30

Written on Sept. 7, 2018

"Dear God,
I love you and I thank you for seeing me through the day. Ultimately, this prayer tonight has to do with the future you have in store for me. Yes, I am still in school, and, don't get me wrong, education is a great resource for so many, but it is the success and rewards of the spirit I now hunger for. As you know, school is something I am good at but not something I look forward to and honestly, I cannot see myself going back year after year. I only seem to do it to pass the time, boost my ego, and because it is simply the 'normal' thing to do at my age. But I do not want to be normal, I have never really been good at it anyway. Point is, I want what you want for me, and if that means school for the time being than I can do that. However, I do desire more; I want to impact people, lead them to you and be an example of an imperfect person serving a perfect God. I thank you in advance for this answered prayer.
In Jesus Name,
Amen."

Your Turn!
Follow Prompt Below

At the time I wrote this prayer, I was 20-years-old with a hunger and thirst for success that was bigger than what I could accomplish on my own. I wanted to make an impact that went beyond a college degree. (*By no means is this a dig at getting an education. But after looking into the motives of why I was doing what I was doing, this letter poured from my heart*). If you are craving something greater than you, take this time to *consult* the Lord about it! Consult: "***seek*** *information or advice from an expert within a* ***specified*** *area."*
Ready? Set. Write.

Now that It Is Written...Read it Aloud!

Prayer #31

"Dear Abba,
I come to you tonight with a thankful heart. You are so awesome, and I continue to be in awe of how you consistently show up in my life. Lord, tonight I lift all the things about myself that I am still perfecting (maturing in). I lift my self-esteem and my lack of confidence in the things that you have placed in me to do. Lord, I pray for my voice and the shyness that always seems to keep me quiet. I pray that you would give me the boldness to speak whenever you tell me to speak like you did with Jeremiah. I pray that you would show me day by day what I am capable of only through you. Lord, help me not to waste the gifts, talents, and abilities that you have given me. Help me to find value in myself and therefore, do what it is that you have assigned me to do. I belong in the board room. My voice is necessary. My abilities are unique and needed. My experiences are an asset to whomever I encounter. I do belong on the committee. I do hold the solution to someone else's problem. Lord, you have placed me here to stop generational inadequacies. Lord, you have anointed me to tear down kingdoms working against your will and build those willing to move forward and promote your Kingdom. I was built for whatever you have strategically planned for my life...both the experiences that feel good to me and the ones that hurt me. I was built and equipped for it all. So Abba, help me to make wiser decisions. I know you gave me the will to do and not to do, and you do not get in the way of that. However, Holy Spirit guide me in this life, so that I may be in the best shape possible to carry out your plans for me. I honor you. I love you and I thank you. Above your name there is no other and I thank you for lending me your ears. I look forward to seeing this petition before you perform in my life. Heaven has heard these words and listened to these decrees and will back me up. Thank you.
In Jesus Mighty Name I Pray,
Amen."

Your Turn!

Follow Prompt Below

Despite our imperfections, the Lord will hide in us the very things He wants to see fulfilled in the earth. Jeremiah was a young boy when the Lord revealed to him that he would be a prophet to the nations. Despite Jeremiah's proclaimed "inadequacies," these were not enough to change God's mind about what he knew of Jeremiah (**Jeremiah 1:4-9**). He will not change His mind toward you either. Take this time to bring those insecurities to God, and pray that He helps you overcome those areas. If you are unsure of where to start, ask Him! Inquire of His thoughts concerning you, and what He may be requiring of you during this season.

Ready? Set. Write.

Now that It Is Written...Read it Aloud!

REFLECTION:

After embarking on this path of prayer and intentional time spent with Jesus, what lesson(s) and realization(s) are you taking with you? Is this something you will continue to do in the future?

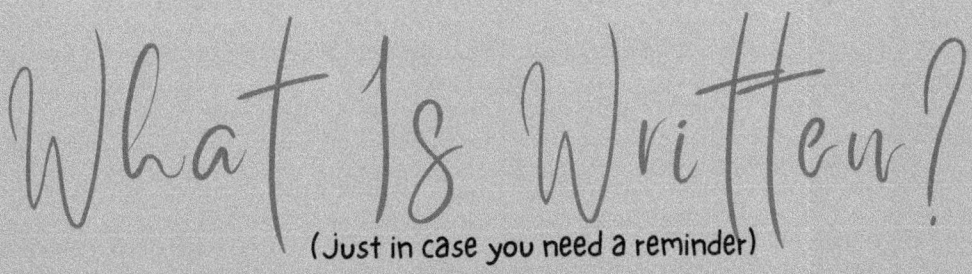

What Is Written?

(Just in case you need a reminder)

"I will not die but live,
and will proclaim what the Lord has
done."
Psalms 118:17

"If God is for me, who can be against me?"
Romans 8:31

"Surely your goodness and love will
follow me
all the days of my life,..."
Psalms 23:6

"For I live by faith, not by sight.."
2 Corinthians 5:7

"No weapon forged against me will prevail."
Isaiah 54:17

"I shall not live by bread alone, but by every word
that comes from the mouth of God."
Matthew 4:4

"Trust in the Lord with all my heart and lean not to my
own understanding. In all my ways acknowledge Him,
and He will direct my paths."
Proverbs 3:5-6

"Greater is He that is in me
than he that is in the world."
1 John 4:4

"The Lord is My Shepherd, I
have everything I need."
Psalms 23:1

"I shall run and not get weary, I shall
walk and not grow faint."
Isaiah 40:31

"He will never leave me
nor forsake me."
Hebrews 13:5

L.T.Y TERMS

Grace: Favor given that is not based on one's good works or efforts, but given freely based solely on the gift of Jesus Christ to the world.

Mercy: Refraining from treating one as their actions deserve. (*For example, instead of God relinquishing his anger on the world which deserved punishment, He put the sins or wrongs of the world on His only son, Jesus instead, saving us from what we were guilty of*).

Holy Spirit: 1 of the 3 components of the Godhead. Jesus was and continues to be the extension and tangible representation of God in human form, making him relatable to you and I. The Holy Spirit is the spirit of God whom was sent to the world when Jesus ascended to be rejoined with the Father after His resurrection. The Holy Spirit is a comforter, helper, and intercessor on our behalf. (*Don't believe God can be 3 in 1? Just look at yourself. You are **spirit**, you live in a **body**, and you have a **soul** that encompasses your will, emotions and intellect*).

Anoint(ed): To consecrate (*dedicate*) or make something sacred to God, often through the use of oil.

Glory: Refers to the weight, importance, honor, splendor, or power of something; often used to describe the presence of God.

Honor: High level of respect or reverence for something or someone.

Shepherd: One who tends to, covers, protects and leads a flock of people or sheep.

Soul: 1 of the 3 components of mankind comprised of their **will** (*what we will/will not do*), **emotions** (*often reinforced my memories*), and **intellect** (*what we know based on knowledge acquired by experience*).

Intercede (Intercession): The action of intervening on behalf of something or someone; also acting as the bridge between the cause and effect. (*For example, the Bible says in Romans 8:26 that when we fail to know what to pray for, the Holy Spirit steps in and makes intercession for us*).

Rebuke: To reprimand or reproach.

Ministry: The expression and spreading of one's faith, often through 1 of the 5 gifts given by God: Apostles, Prophets, Evangelists, Pastors, and Teachers.

Steadfast: To do something dutifully with unwavering tenacity and loyalty.

Endow: To provide or equip something or someone with the ability to do something.

Righteousness: Being in right standing with God. (*Our own righteousness are as filthy rags according to Isaiah 64:6, this is why we lean on the righteousness of God and why we are encouraged to pursue His righteousness in Matthew 6:33*).

Ordain: To decree, appoint, anoint or order something.

Prevail: To withstand any opposing forces or win against all odds.

Principality: An area ruled by one in authority, such as a prince.

L.T.Y TERMS CONT.

Predestined: An outcome that is already divinely determined or known.

Convict (conviction): To be made known or aware of wrongdoing or error within oneself. This is a result of having the Holy Spirit.

Cast: To give away, usually referring to cares, concerns, worries and internal turmoil.

RAYLA'S PLAYLIST

Aside from prayer, music has become another go-to for me, and there have been many songs that have kept me going, strengthened my faith, and elevated my spirit to a place of tranquility and understanding. Listed below are just a few of the songs and albums that have helped me over the years. I am praying they also be a help and inspiration to you.

"Throne Room" (Full Album)– Cece Winans

"I Desire More"– Crystal Akin

"Jireh"– Maverick City

"The Blood"– Naomi Raine

"Be the Place"– Naomi Raine

"Forth" (Full Album)– V. Rose"

"You're the Lifter"– Ricky Dillard

"Wait on You"– Elevation Worship & Maverick City

"Here as in Heaven"– Elevation Worship

"So Will I"– Osby Berry

"I Will Exalt You"– Darrel Walls

"Yahweh"– All Nations

"Breathe/What a Friend I've Found"– Hillsong Worship

"Vet" (Full Album)– Da' T.R.U.T.H.

"Respond"– Travis Greene

"Love is an Action Word" (Full Album)– Witness

"The Lord's Song"– Maranda Curtis

"The Blessing" –Kari Jobe and Cody Carnes (Elevation Worship)

"Alpha and Omega Session"– WorshipMob live with Cross Worship

"Yeshua"– Jesus Image

"Us Against the World" (Full Album)– David and Tamera Mann

"Revelation 19:1"– Naomi Raine & Mav City Gospel Choir

"Too Good To Not Believe"– Brandon Lake

"I Will Remember"– K.J. Scriven

"A New Thing" (Full Album)– Madison Ryann Ward

"Hallelujah Here Below"– Elevation Worship feat. Steffany Gretzinger